A Heart Story

He held her heart
in his hands and she
wasn't entirely certain
if he would drop it
break it or just keep it
safe with him
but for now she just loved
the feel of his hands there.

- N.R. Hart

"What is love"

What is love, you ask? Love is a
complicated little beast.
But, allow me to simplify it for you.
Love is the way you look at someone,
not just looking, but knowing them,
seeing into their soul.
Love is being there...and always feeling safe
with them.
Love is sensing what they need without
them having to ask.
Love is pure acceptance...all your
flaws, your scars, your secrets.
Love is the easiest thing in the world
to know, to show, to do. But, we make it
hard. Hard to hold onto. We get in our
own way. Because love is many things...but,
in the end, love is just someone who
doesn't have to understand you but
somehow, tries to. Love is someone who doesn't
give up on you. Because, love is
unconditional. Because, love is constant.
Because, love stays.   -N.R.Hart

Poetry of her heart

She clutched her books
ever so tightly
holding them dear to her.
They were the poetry
of her heart, after all.
And, you will never know
how much courage it took
to write them.
It came with a price,
you know...
baring her soul.

—N.R.Hart

Because they don't think
like you do, dear girl.
If you love them
really love them
you choose them
over everything else
but, they never choose you
do they?
And this is why you
write about love.
Because it doesn't exist
anywhere but in your mind
and the ink on this paper.

                    -N.R.Hart

                              "Spilled ink"

I loved you
and you loved me
we lost it somehow
this precious thing
we held so high
and protected
with all our might
I gripped you tight
and tighter still
but you loosened yours
our precious thing
And down down down
we fell.
.N.R.Hart

She romanticized you
penned sonnets of verse
and rhyme
loving all of you
madly, ceaselessly
and now you know
this was no ordinary love
and now you see you will
live without this
throughout all time.

N.R.Hart

Old Soul

I am an old soul living in the
wrong century.
I want genuine conversation.
I want to look into your eyes
when we are speaking.
To see your heart and feel your
soul.
I want romance. I want deep.
I want real.
True connection that has become
a lost art in a modern world.

N.R.Hart ©

The greatest love stories
never came easy. They are
the ones you fight for
because you can't imagine
life without them.
So instead of easy
the only love for her
was the persistent can't
stop thinking about them
kind of love. A love she
couldn't deny.
        -N.R.Hart

Queen

She was a queen
but he settled for a pauper.
She was a diamond
he let slip through his hands.
A girl like her
all heart and soul
she was pure gold.
But, he settled for less
because he didn't believe
in himself.

                    -N.R.Hart

Brave girl

He said, brave girl I know
you are tired.
You don't have to be
so strong all the time.
I want you to know you are
not alone because I am not
going anywhere.
And, with that he took her
into his arms as she laid
her head on his shoulder.
She finally allowed herself
to rest.
She stayed there for the
longest time just listening to
the safe sound of him staying.

-N.R.Hart , Brave girl

"Captive"

And, I began to
breathe easier
with you...
all the breaths
held captive
inside me...
were set free.

-N.R.Hart

She was always told
she could be
whatever
she wanted...
so she mustered up
every ounce of courage
she had and decided
to just be herself...
and she was finally happy
and she was finally free.

-N.R.Hart "free" ©

19

"This romance"

You and me...
we will survive this
romance?
We know nothing of what
is to be yet,
This is all I want.
You are all I see.

-N.R.Hart

"deeply"

It never mattered
to her to be loved
by everyone
it only mattered
to her to be loved
deeply...
by someone.

-N.R.Hart

Disenchanted

I always thought there was
so much more to you
so much more...
than there actually was.
I worshipped the ground
you walked on.
How disappointing to find out
that you weren't
any of those things...
And, I was wrong.

N.R.Hart, disenchanted

You love with everything
you have...
not everyone possesses
that kind of courage.

N.R.Hart   "Courage"

Your eyes breathe
things
and I am at a loss
for words...
I only know I can find
your soul in them.

N.R.Hart , find your soul

24

"Healer"

All she had were her words
to give them...
she found them buried deep
in her bones
she bared everything for them
so she could ease their pain...
make them feel less alone.
She wanted to comfort them
heal their souls...
so they wouldn't carry that pain
home.   -N.R.Hart

She's a deadly combination
of innocent and sexy
black velvet eyes
soft and wild
she's a heartbreaker
of a girl
you just hang on for the ride
and hope you'll survive.

N.R.Hart, Heartbreaker

26

How often we rely
on hope alone
to get us through
the day
to keep our hearts
beating.
Hope is a powerful thing.
Hope can keep you alive.

-N.R.Hart (Hope Can Keep You Alive)

"Her Love Story"

Her story wasn't just any love story
the way she fought for love
lived and died for love
she was fearless in love...
A romantic girl by nature.
A real heartbreaker.   N.R.Hart
A beauty who turns men into beasts.
A girl who follows her heart
to the ends of the earth
if she loves you.
The kind of love story that will
go down in history.
She will make her mark on this world.
Because of her, love hasn't been
the same since...
She made certain of that.   -N.R.Hart

"

Don't ever deny your true
passions
even when others don't
understand you.
Never explain yourself...
They will either dance
in your flames
or wallow in the ashes.
Keep burning.

-N.R.HART "KEEP BURNING"

I want to love what I was meant
to love in this world
and I know I was meant
to love you.

N.R.Hart, Beauty and her Beast ©

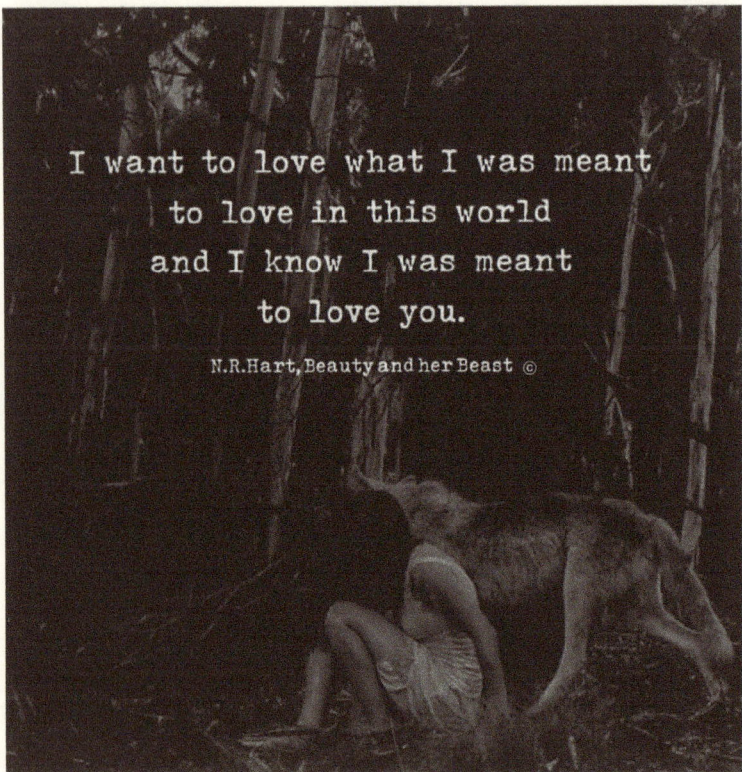

"Love of your life"
I knew I was in trouble
it felt all too familiar
a best friend
always meant to be
he was the male version
of me...
it's why I understood him
so well
it was like watching myself.
How does he not know it?
How does he not see?
I was a version of him too...
The love of your life is simply
a version of you.

N.R.Hart, Love of your Life

31

Silence

There is nothing so

deafening as the silence

between two souls...

who are still in love

with each other.

-N.R.Hart, The Last of the
                Romantics

The Universe

It was the way they looked
at each other.
Most days they couldn't take
their eyes off each other.
Most days words weren't even
necessary.
Because their souls had a secret
language all their own.
No matter how much time had
passed between them
there was still that burning excitement.
And, every time felt like
the first time.
A love as big as the sky
as hot as the sun
as deep as the sea.
Because, a love that was old
and new, familiar and exciting,
all at once.
To talk about it felt, small.
They were larger than life.
They were inevitable.
The beginning and The end. -N.R.Hart

There is no in-between
with me
when I love, I love.
My whole heart and soul
are yours for the taking.
Before you give your love away
be certain they possess
the same fire
the same passion
the same depth.
Make sure they have
the same heart as yours,
my darling.
Because, they don't love
like you love.
Because, you will always be
the one who loves more.

-N.R.Hart (they don't love like you love)

Warrior Princess

Her heart was a romantic
warrior princess
no matter how many times
she lost the battle
in love
she never gave up
the fight.

                    -N.R.Hart

"Memories"

You can try to forget but, you and I
both know our story lives on and on...
every word, every line, every rhyme
we lived it. We breathed it.
We felt it. We still do.....
A love so rare, a passion so alive
a fire branding our souls for a
lifetime.
Nothing else compares.
How can we forget when we gave each
other so much to remember?
Your heart racing next to mine.
Memories so deep, embedded in our hearts,
our eyes, our minds...
Where it will stay haunting us
throughout all time.
You can run far but you can never
outrun "us". You can never outrun love.
Because, some love stories never die.
Because, these memories live inside...
burning you alive. -N.R.Hart

"she awoke one day
only to find pieces of herself
in everything she had ever
loved.
and, this is why she never felt
whole again...but somehow,
it was enough."

-N.R.Hart

The purpose of life
is to know yourself
to love yourself
unconditionally
and, most importantly
to be yourself.

        -N.R.Hart

But, my darling
you being
different...
was your strength
all along.
                    —N. R. Hart

She began each day fearless
breaking hearts and slaying dragons
love and chaos both her weakness
and her strength.

-N.R.Hart

She loved too much and you
could see it by the fragile
look in her eyes...
for she knew just how precious
her burden was...
carrying all those hearts.

-N.R.Hart "precious"

"Love a romantic girl
and you will have
an endless love affair."

-N.R.Hart

And then one day
she finally realized
that no matter what
she said or did
how hard she tried
she couldn't save
everyone...
Not even herself. -N.R.Hart

The poets are not the popular
ones, they are the loners,
the misunderstood ones
and most people keep their distance
because the poets
speak of the hard truths
they don't want to hear,
because the poets see
into their souls...
They understand energy. They notice
everything. When something is off they
know it. They are the empaths, the
vulnerable ones who feel too much
in a world that does not know how to.
They are the romantics who suffer
for love, for others...
turning everything into something
beautiful.
They want so badly to believe love
conquers all. And, how this world keeps
disappointing them
with its brutal reality.

N.R.Hart   "the Poets"

Mermaids

She is the strange beautiful girl
the one they don't understand
the one they are afraid of...
Her love runs deep
the kind of deep simple men
drown in...
and when they finally catch their breath
they realize...
girls like her were mermaids
drowning you in a sea of love
strong enough to save you.

-N.R.Hart, Sea of Love (mermaids)

She is a beautiful chaos
a rebellious lover
tragically romantic
passionately savage
innocent and serene
never judge a book
by its cover
the secrets are hidden
from within
because things are never
as they seem. -N.R.Hart

"She was in love
with love
and she never understood
how the rest of the world
wasn't in love
the way she was."

-N.R.Hart

"So gather up your brilliant
and shining pieces
you will show them
how broken becomes beautiful."

-N.R.Hart, The Last of the Romantics

My relentless pursuit
of love
passion, poetry...
in all its grandeur
will also be
my greatest tragedy.

-N.R.Hart, The Last of the
           Romantics

A Spring Season

"And, loving... is an art, too."

N.R.Hart

I am a romantic
a lover
a dreamer...
and this will be
the very death
of me.

-N.R.Hart

The Last of the Romantics N.R.Hart °2016

51

Romance & Rebellion

"But every girl needs a little romance and rebellion."

N.R.Hart

She never seemed to be
on the same page
as the others
her mind always somewhere else
far far away
in a different land
a different chapter
in a completely different
book
one she wrote herself.

N.R.Hart , A Different Book One She Wrote Herself

A Legendary Love Story (part2)

A love story from which legends
are made of
passed down through centuries
of Shakespeare and Keats and Bronte.
A charming boy who spelled trouble
a witty girl who fell hard.
A most poetic love story indeed.
A story of how fate brought them
together and how life tore them
apart.
How she loves him desperately and
has her heart broken by him.
She is destroyed when he leaves
until he realizes too late
that they were always meant to be.
And, how they loved one another.
Still.
And yet, the most awful truth...
They would have to live without
each other in the end.   -N.R.Hart

The Last of the Romantics© 2021

54

I never understood those
who can love so frivolously
giving their hearts away
to just anyone at all.
I watch them and I think
how dreadful to love
so quickly?
The only love for me
is a soul love
or the love will not stay
long.
            -N.R.Hart, soul love

i clung to you in ways i did not
understand...
i clung to your darkness and
the light in your eyes
i clung to your hands
and the way they made me feel
vulnerable...
i clung to you in every way possible
because you made me feel alive.
—n.r.hart "alive"

All I want
all I really want...
is to just keep talking
to you
and it doesn't matter what
we talk about
as long as you
are with me.
Just be with me...
And, we can figure out the rest
later.
- N.R.Hart

She looks at you
with that fire
in her eyes
and somehow
you just know
you'll never
make it out alive
yet, you go in
anyway...-N.R.Hart

She was never cautious
when it came to love
when she loves she loves hard
surrendering her heart, her soul.
Love makes you vulnerable
it is dangerous and holds
the power to destroy you.
There is no restraint with love,
no self-control. Love is chaotic
love is crazy and passionate.
It makes you lose control.
And if it is not these things
then...you haven't experienced
a true love at all. -N.R.Hart

"castles"

I built castles
in your eyes
and dreams in your smile
and I don't know how
to wake up from
this fairytale love.   -N.R.Hart

I wanted to see you
because my eyes still
look for you.
I wanted to touch you
but your hands
are too far away.
I wanted to tell you
I miss you
but my heart is too afraid.
Why is it the words
that mean the most
are the hardest to say.

-N.R.Hart (hardest to say)

"enchanted"

The only thing I could
hear
was the beating of my
own heart
the only thing I could
feel
was the crashing
of our two souls
you were mesmerizing
and I was enchanted
and the rest of the world
just...disappeared. -N.R.Hart

In over my head

I knew the moment I laid eyes on you
that you were going to be trouble.
Everything about you felt familiar.
Everything about you felt right.
The connection was a powerful one...a strong
magnetic pull of the Universe.   N.R.Hart
I couldn't run even if I wanted to. And, I
thought this one feels different somehow,
because I felt completely vulnerable with you.
I couldn't catch my breath with you.
I knew I was in over my head and didn't care
in the least about the danger I was in.
The danger of losing my heart to you.
The way you stole my soul and made it yours.
I was putty in your hands and I knew I was
going to love you in a way I have never loved
anyone.
How you would own every piece of me each one
screaming your name.
This one was dangerous because this one held
the power to destroy me.
As I stood there with my eyes watching
my own demise.   -N.R.Hart

The Last of the Romantics

I wanted you in the most
basic of ways
I wanted you
eye to eye
soul to soul
skin on skin
your heart beating
next to mine
our bodies melting
into each other
I want you now and forever.
I want you always.

-N.R.Hart

There is a sort of magic
that occurs
when you first lay eyes
on someone
something inside you
clicks
and in that moment
you just know they are
meant to be important
in your life somehow...
And, nothing will ever
be the same again. -N.R.Hart

"little nothings"

Like a girl with a heart
full of little nothings
i tell you sweet things
i tell you silly things
and you just sit there
listening with your eyes
and smile back at me
with that look
of yours...
the one that i live for
the one that i die for.

-N.R.Hart

Quietly

And, that was the thing
about us.
We needed each other...
quietly.
We didn't talk about it...
but it was there.
Even when we didn't know it...
it was somehow understood.
Even when I was the only one
to notice...
It was still so.   -N.R.Hart

Map to my soul

Looking at you, hurt.
Your little quirks
your idiosyncrasies
the things no one ever notices.
The things only I get to see.
To me, you look vulnerable
and sweet and sometimes sad.
The familiar outline of the child
you once were.
I catch my breath...
I find it hard to breathe
at all.
Your eyes stole my heart.
You are so perfect for me.
Like a map to my soul.
I love you so hard...
Looking at you, hurt. -N.R.Hart

WHY ARE THINGS SWEETER
ONCE THEY ARE LOST
I WISH WE COULD
GO BACK IN TIME
WHEN YOU WERE MINE.
WHY DID YOU NOT SEE
HOW PRECIOUS I WAS
WHEN YOU HAD ME.
-N.R.HART

my heart needs your heart

I like the way you pay
attention to me
how you stop everything
just to look at me...
I need to tell you
everything in my heart.
Because you are the one
person I want to tell
things to.
Because my heart...
it needs your heart.

-N.R.Hart

Scent

She willingly follows him
responding to his call
of the wild.
Longing for the beast in him
by night he owns her like
no one ever could...
her body breathing
only where he touches her.
Their hearts already know
the way
their souls have been here
before...
his scent leads her home.

-N.R.Hart

"Restless"

I am so restless for you...
Fancy me as the dew drops
on lily pads
screaming out for the heat
of the sun to burn through
my skin.
Fancy me as a flock of snapdragons
swaying to the soft breeze
crying out to be picked and held
on fiery display.
Fancy me as the screeching
of butterflies swirling in unison
to the blades of grass flying into
the arms of the summer sky.
Fancy me as all these things...
the sweet ache of passion and desire.
Because, I too, am so restless for you.

              -N.R.Hart

A secret place
a secret love
somewhere only
we know of
when it was just
you and me
where we could love
wild and free.
-N.R.Hart

Reckless heart

Her heart was reckless
around him
she couldn't help herself
she craved everything about him...
his boyish charm, his devastating
smile
rendering her helpless.
She needed his silence, his chaos,
his company. She needed him.
It was all so unexplainable and so very
reckless...
She was under his spell
her pulse quickening, her breathing
unsteady...
surrendering herself over to him.
Whatever the danger, not once did her
reckless heart
ask to be saved from the start.

-N.R.Hart

Unbreakable

When they ask me about you
I could never really explain
it...explain us.
How even after all the love
and the madness
the joy and the heartbreak
I still could not let go of you.
What they did not understand
was the bond between us
that was created long ago.
We were an ancient love
older than any love story
ever told.
Where it remains invincible.
It goes well beyond the physical realm
and resides somewhere deep
in the soul dimension.
We were fragile, you and I,
so very fragile.
And yet, we were unbreakable. -N.R.Hart

N.R.Hart

The Truth about Love

He said to her
love me more...
But don't you know by now
darling,
she already loves you...
she is just fearful
of loving you more
because that is what
she does best.
Loving more...
For once she wanted
someone to love her.
More.
          -N.R.Hart

"The Last of the Romantics" by N.R.Hart

"Romance is not dead"
They say romance is dead
and I say romance is very much
alive...
At least to the romantics, it is.
Believing in romanticism is not an easy
thing in this lifeless world.
Being a romantic is about seeing the
optimism where there is none.
It's finding beauty in the face of boredom.
It's rebellion in the comfort of conformity.
It's living instead of dying.
The very essence of romanticism is the
sweet torment for the fervor of passion
almost torturous; to feel it...to live it...
And, what true romantics suffer for.
Romanticism is bravery.
It is from another place, another
dimension.
Ancient, timeless, chivalry at its finest.
Shakespeare and Keats. Lord Byron and
Bronte.
Romance is found in all the hidden places
others never bother to look.
This is why romantics become lost...
in poetry, in love, in life. -N.R.Hart

You cupped my face
in your hands
and kissed me hard
time stood still
as my body burst
into flames
wherever you touched me
your burning kiss
leaving a mark
for all eternity.

N.R.Hart, Burning Kiss

They drove for hours
in the rain
just listening to music
her head leaning
on his shoulder
his hands playing
with her hair
as the day raced by
he felt like safe freedom
to her...
he was all soothing eyes
and pretty melodies
she was all sweet kisses
and warm fire.

N.R.Hart,   Pretty Melodies

The Moon The Stars The Sea

He looked over at her. And, he thought to
himself, this girl is something special.
He never met anyone like her before.
She seemed ethereal to him...
like the moon or the stars or the sea.
Her light spread out around him.
Her warmth covered him just by sitting
next to her. Had he been in the dark this whole
time? He was intrigued by her.
He wanted to devour her whole...her mind,
her soul.
As luck would have it, he was a persistent man.
A patient wolf.
He had all the time in the world for her.
She was smart and shy and beautiful and
sexy, a most interesting combination.
She was a breath of fresh air. She spoke in
poetry and metaphors. She was deliciously
complicated. Foolish men might otherwise rush
to get to her surface, but he was after so
much more. He wanted to learn her, study her.
Speak her language.
He saw that fire in her eyes...he was melting
in that fire...he didn't want to play with it,
he wanted to burn in it.   -N.R.Hart

"Still"

You are still searching for me
searching for that soul love in everyone
you meet.
Kisses so deep you can still taste my name
on your lips and how you hunger for that
now.
You still listen for my laugh when you
crack your silly jokes because their laugh
doesn't tease you, egg you on, the way mine
did.   N.R.Hart
You still look for my eyes and our quiet
understanding that we shared in all the
empty stares, the replacements you keep
trying hard to fill but, only one love
burns your soul forever.
You still feel my hands all over you,
touching you, exciting you, needing you
and now, you are left wanting more.
Because a frienship so alive, a passion
that never dies only comes once in a
lifetime.
And, still you seach for me in everyone
you see.
But, you will never replace me. -N.R.Hart

81

I have seen those parts
of you
I have breathed and
touched those beautiful
and secret parts of you
that you refuse to show.
And, that taste
it stays with you forever.

-N. R. Hart

it's spring here
It's spring here sweetheart
do you ever think of me
like I think of you?
The sweet sweet spring
pink and blue flowers
and poplar trees and honey bees
strolling through fields of green
hand in hand
warm kisses in the car,
in the grass, in your arms
so many kisses in the wild sunlight
under the tender moonlight
do you ever think of me
when you hear a country song
and how we used to sing along,
do you? Do you?
It's spring here sweetheart and
I miss you. I miss you. -N.R.Hart

Seasons

I wanted all of her
he said...
her spring and her
summer
her fall and her winter.
I wanted all her
seasons...
her light and her dark
everyone wanted a piece
of her
and, he just wanted her
heart.

N.R.Hart, Seasons

dragon girl

But, there is a reason
why you are different
and others fear what
they do not understand
you are a dragon
of a girl
breathing fire
and they have never even
been warm.

N.R.Hart dragon girl

She was strong
and fragile
brave and vulnerable,
all at once.

-N.R.Hart

"Tea party"

She was a quiet girl
a thoughtful girl
but you were never
quite sure what was
going on inside that
pretty little head
of hers.
Was it planning her next
tea party;
or a plot to take over
the world?
                    -N.R.Hart

I thought to tell you
so many things
but when it all comes
down to it
all those other things
never really mattered
when all I was trying
to say was...I love you.
I love you. I love you.

-N.R.Hart (I love you)

oh, dear one
why are you so
helpless
when it comes to your
own heart. why?

-N.R.Hart

Rose Garden

She planted a garden
in me
her sweet roots twisted
inside my ribcage
full of roses and hyacinths
butterflies and fire.
I wander all day
breathing her in...
hers is the only perfume
I remember.
N.R.Hart, Perfume

A springtime
fancy
my soul
blooms love
and poetry...
I am only alive
then.

-N.R.Hart

"Their souls were always
touching
like twin flames.
Existing within each other
and burning through
everything else.

-N.R.Hart "Twin Flames"

Soulmate poem

During your lifetime there
will be one person who is
unlike any other. You will
know this because you feel
different around them. You feel
more like yourself because you
can sense them deep in your soul.
They make you feel more alive.
You can tell them anything
and their love for you is
unconditional.
This person is your best friend
and your soulmate.
You will not find anyone like
them again. Never let them go.

-N.R.Hart, Soulmate Poem

Shakespearean Tragedy

She is intensely
passionate
devastatingly romantic
mysteriously complicated
like a Shakespearean
tragedy
not something everyone can
comprehend.

-N.R.Hart

The Rose

Sometimes, I am in awe of my own words
how brave they are...are they braver
than me?
How they tell a story, my story...
of the person trapped inside of me.
Because, there are some days I am
uncertain, so uncertain...of all this
love living inside me. All this hope
keeping me alive...
How my words are breathing and
breaking, all at once...
Always loving the beautiful things.
The sad things. The impossible things.
Some days I am the wildflower
following the flutterings of my own
heart.
And, other days I am the wallflower
drowning in the dying light.
Just let me be the rose...
all petals and thorns, both soft and
strong. Let me love hard.
Let me survive it all. -N.R.Hart

The Last of the Romantics©

95

The Romance

I like the anticipation that
leads up to love...
the flirting, the teasing
the touching
then the passion
the hurried breaths
the groping, the feeling
the kissing...
hands and mouths everywhere.
The anticipation of it all.
The romance of it all.

-N.R.Hart ©

Maybe I love
too much
and I show it
way too much
but I would rather
be too much than
too little.

-N.R.Hart

If she had to choose between
the prince and the beast
the answer would be both;
she wants the valiant knight
in armor to protect her
while summoning the wild beast
inside to love her.

N.R. Hart, *Beauty and her Beast* ©2019

And, she scares all
the boys away
she is a wildfire
to their match
some have tried to hold
a candle to her flame...
when will they learn
she waits for the one
who isn't afraid to
burn.   -N.R.Hart

When will love
fight for her

She is so tired
of fighting for what
she loves
she is strong but
she is tired.
When will love fight
for her. When?

-N.R.Hart

100

A Summer Season

"Just love her, wildly."

N.R.Hart

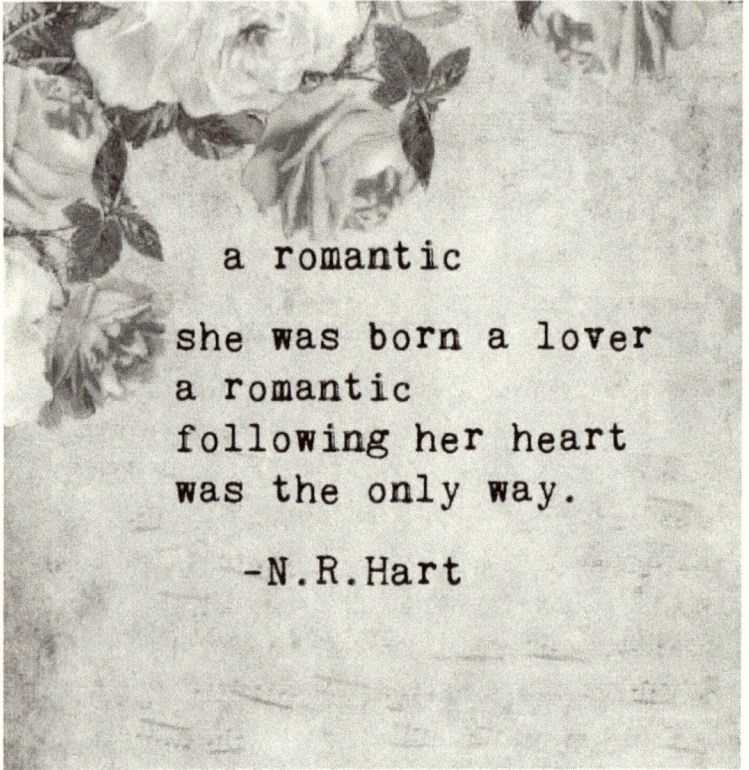

a romantic

she was born a lover
a romantic
following her heart
was the only way.

-N.R.Hart

She didn't show herself
to many
how could they fathom
the fervor of passion
burning her
from the inside out
when most run
from the smoke
for they were the timid ones.
And after all,
she was all fire.
-N.R.Hart

"

How do you know
the difference
between loving someone
and being in love...
with someone?
My dear, one is simply rain
the other...
A hurricane.

N.R.HART, "A HURRICANE"

FIRE

WHAT SCARES HER
THE MOST IS
WHAT IF NO ONE
TOUCHES
ALL THIS FIRE
SHE HIDES INSIDE.

-N.R.HART

i always think about you
when i am driving in my car
music blaring, stars above
i am free moving in the wind
just like falling and flying
all at once...with you.
—nrhart

It's the connection to
someone the friendship...
that makes you feel
comforted.
True love is born from true
intimacy.
Because losing a lover is
bad
but losing your best friend
is worse.

—N.R.Hart "Intimacy"

I am not certain of many things
yet, I am certain of love,
of passion, of lust
of romance...
These are the things that rule
me in life. Nothing else.
I want to be the one who changes
your breathing.
The reason you can't sleep at night.
I want to feel the heat of passion
the madness of lust
the pounding of my heart.
I want only this.
And I want it with you.

  -N.R.Hart, The Last of the Romantics

Feed her hunger as only
a wolf can
strip her bare
wearing only your scent
bathed in moonlight
claw marks upon silken flesh
pierce her soul raw and
ravenous.
Insatiable for your love
leave no part of her
untouched.
She desires the animal in you
sink your teeth into her and
take
what is yours.

-N.R.Hart "Hunger"

Disturb the Universe

I find myself inhaling you
how long have I been
holding this breath?
afraid to exhale
afraid to disturb
the Universe
afraid to lose
the rest of you
and I don't know
how long I can
go on breathing
for you...for us.

-N.R.Hart

Dragon love

Once you get a taste of her.
The sweetest sin.
The deepest kiss.
The hottest fuck.
The endless romance...
There is no going back is there?
Addicted to the good bad girl.
Everything else pales
in comparison...   N.R.Hart
You can't get her out of your head
from underneath your skin
her heat coursing through your
veins.
The purest kind of dragon love...
Fire seeping from every pore.
Your mouth still watering from
the taste of her.

N.R.Hart "Dragon Love" © 2016

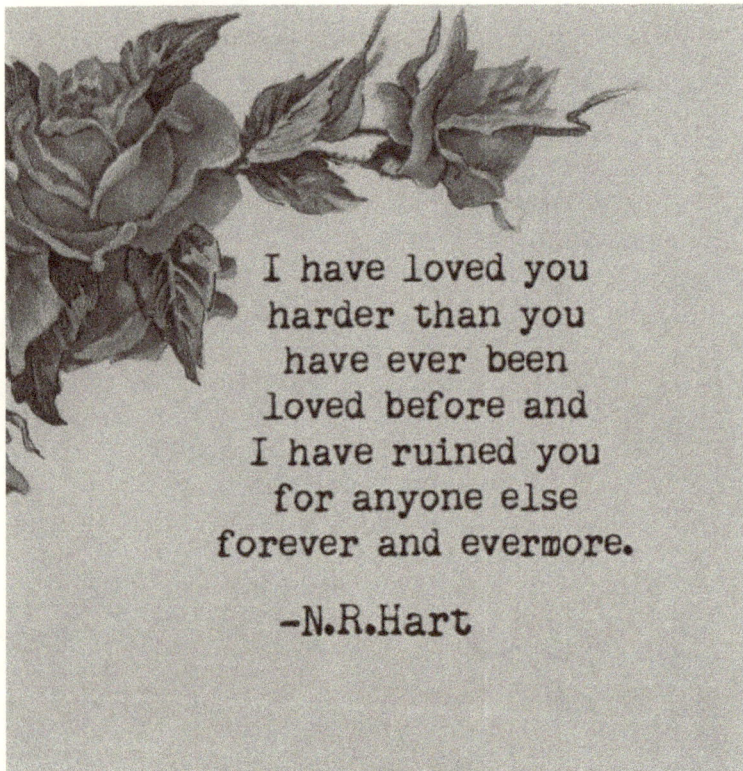

I have loved you
harder than you
have ever been
loved before and
I have ruined you
for anyone else
forever and evermore.

-N.R.Hart

Restless soul

I am looking for a restless soul
like mine
give me someone with
a beautiful mind and wild eyes
a passionate lover with
a burning kiss
who will tear down my walls
with their bare hands
just to make love to my naked
vulnerability.
And, please...
Let them be fearless.

-N.R.Hart

Soul Kiss

He said...I am going
to
kiss you
so that you feel it
deep in
your soul
until you become weak
in the knees
I will make you forget

everything...
but me.
And, with one kiss...he made
a believer
out of her. Just like that.

N.R.Hart "soul kiss"

114

I love you because my soul never forgets (part II)

Here is what I remember most...
The way your eyes were the sweetest
most vulnerable part of you.
You don't know this but it was your
eyes that spoke to me...
I heard words behind your eyes
the way they watched me
followed me, chased me...
How your eyes would flirt with me.
Could you hear my heart pounding
every time you looked at me?
And, in-between each kiss...
how you caught my breath in your
mouth.
I swear I could taste your soul on my
lips...
I remember that you were my true love.
My truest love. My deepest love.
My soul love.
I love you because my soul never forgets.
                    -N.R.Hart

N.R.Hart

"good girls"

Maybe I am the good girl.
But, no one has ever made
me feel the way that you do.
So I tend to lose my mind
a little with you.
I tend to lose my mind
a lot with you.
Everything I know goes out
the door.
So baby, remember this...
If I ever get you alone
all to myself...I will
shut that door behind me
and lock it myself.

-N.R.Hart

It was a hot summer night
you are driving and my hand
is inside yours.
Your skin felt warm and the heat
between us becomes unbearable.
You pull over reaching for me
your mouth on mine and our hands
groping each other
as you pick me up placing me
on the hood taking me right there
loving me deep loving me hard
and the only sound is my body
screaming your name. -N.R.Hart

Hellfire kisses

You lost her and it wasn't
because you didn't love her
instead,
you were scared of her love
scared of your feelings
for her
of not being in control
of a love that made you
feel too much....
You can keep your ordinary love
with your ordinary kisses.
I only want kisses from
hellfire
and a thunderous love
cracking my heart in two.
I only ever wanted you. -N.R.Hart

She was soft
as an angel
but oh,
she could love with
the fury of a demon.

-N.R.Hart

Best Friends

He was my best friend
I had a crush on
he meant everything
so I kissed him
and,
my soul cracked open
my whole world went down
in flames.

-N.R.Hart

"I know it's a dangerous thing
to want you like
this...
but, here I am
wanting you."

-N.R.Hart

I want to feel
the tenderness
when he holds my hand
the heat
as he is touching me
the playfulness
tugging at my hair
the wickedness
as he slides his hand
up my skirt
and the roughness
when he takes me.
-N.R.Hart   (A man's hands)

In the right hands
she becomes
something else...
a sweetheart gone rogue
something soft
something wild.
In the right hands
she melts.

-N.R.Hart "gone rogue"

I wonder where you are tonight
 as I sit here all alone
I tried so many ways to tell you
yet my secret is still unknown
you're so far away but oh,
how I wanted you to know
how long I have waited to love you
and tell you so.
-N.R.Hart

Sometimes you just want to be
grabbed and kissed
long and hard.
If she is looking at you,
I mean really gazing into
your eyes without looking away
then she is dying for you to
kiss her...
Don't hesitate. She wants a man
who can possess her, take control
of her, make her his.
Push her up against the wall,
manhandle her a bit and kiss her
deliberately.
She wants to be taken by you.
            —N.R.Hart

"the art of kissing a woman"

Legend of wolf and moon

she was like the moon
and he, her wolf
always circling
his shadow cast in her
moonlight
waiting for love
to break free
with the stars.

                    -N.R.Hart

126

Love lived there

And, she loved him in ways
she could barely fathom
it took root inside her
dwelling in her dark fields
and sunlit valleys;
the way it made a home
inside her
devouring her whole.
Love lived there, she could
feel it.
It was deep in her bones.
In her soul.

-N.R.Hart

Leather and Lace

I try to pretend
these feelings
don't exist
yet every thought
ties into you
every touch
unravels me
you get tangled up
inside this
leather and lace
I can't help but
come undone.

                    —N. R. Hart

I want to feel
your hands
gripping my hair
your mouth
crushing down hard
on mine
the sweet sting
of your fingers
upon my flesh.
Make your mark on me.
Love me like you mean it.
Love me like you own me.
Leave me aching
for more.

-N.R.Hart   "Love Me"

Love you again

You are the love
that keeps returning
to me.
The love that won't
go away.
You are the love
that stays.
I let go while
still holding on...
god, how I want to
love you again.

-N.R.Hart

She kissed him goodnight
and slid out the door
how she wanted to linger
some more
to kiss him again
and show him her love
oh, how she longed
to stay with him that night
loving him was easy
loving him felt right.
-N.R.Hart

Midnight

Come for me at midnight
when the moon is full
and the air thick with lust
while the heat is in my bones
hurry, come love me tonight.

-N.R.Hart

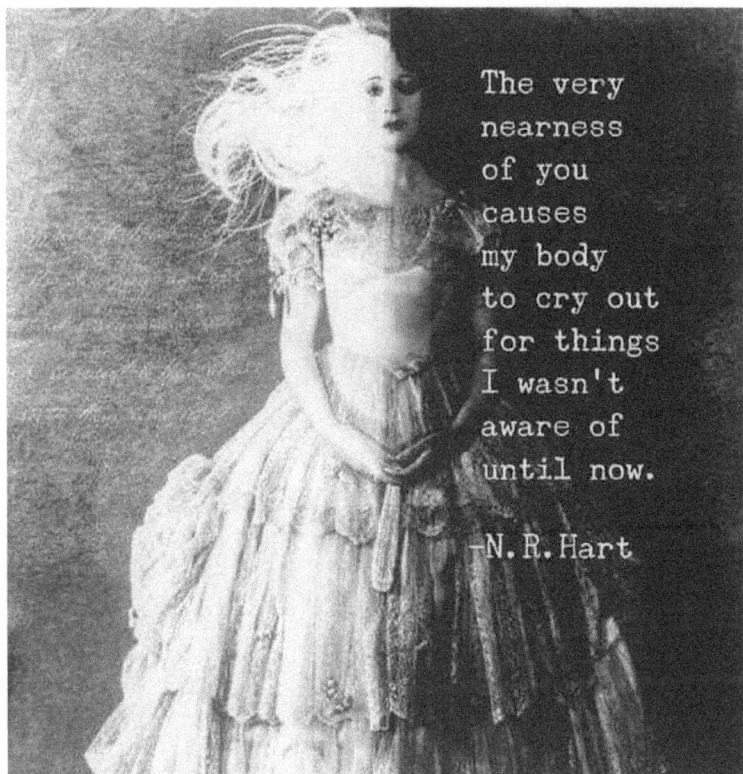

The very
nearness
of you
causes
my body
to cry out
for things
I wasn't
aware of
until now.

-N. R. Hart

I am worth it.
And, it's too bad
you didn't have
the courage to fight
for me.
I only want the kind
of love
worth fighting for
or none at all.

-N.R.Hart, worth it

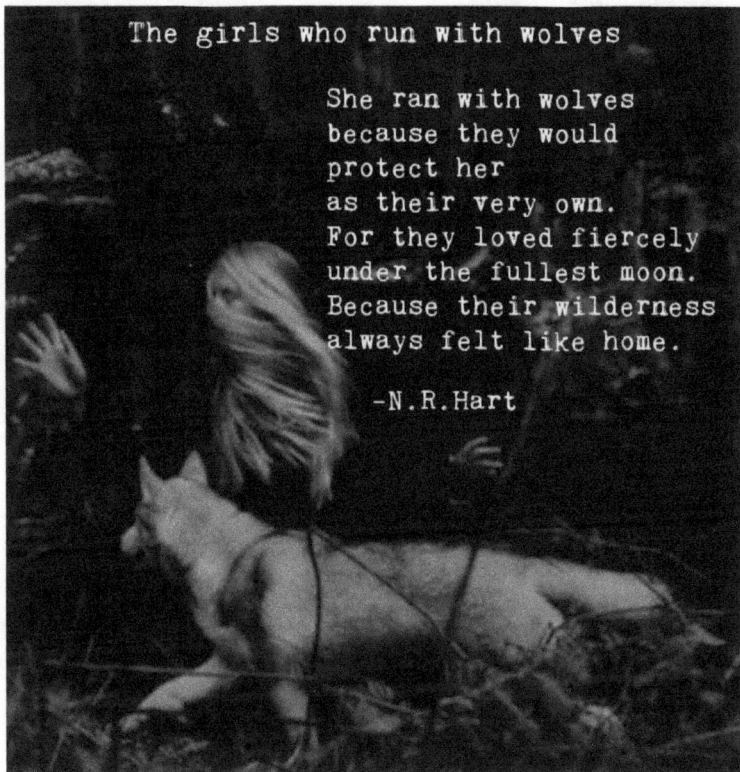

The girls who run with wolves

She ran with wolves
because they would
protect her
as their very own.
For they loved fiercely
under the fullest moon.
Because their wilderness
always felt like home.

-N.R.Hart

135

Soul Lovers

It wasn't like we could control it
it was always there between us
this deep connection
this strong physical attraction
this intense chemistry.
A powerful emotional bond
connected by an invisible red string
and though this string had been
pulled to its breaking point
it never breaks, it never does.
This twin energy of the universe
keeps us spiritually and soulfully
connected. Unable to control it,
it controls us instead.
We were soul lovers.
We were the lovers our bodies
always remember.
We were the lovers our souls
never forget.

N. R. Hart, Soul Lovers

It was a hot summer day
I could still feel your warmth
next to me
the way your fingers pressed
into my skin
how they moved across me
there was music in your hands
as you drove
playing me like a song
and how you never left
an inch of me
untouched....
I still feel you there.
I still feel you everywhere.
I try to convince myself
I'm not in love with you
anymore...
only to realize I still was.
(I still am.)

N.R.Hart , The Truth About Love

Slay

Her heart is in
a constant battle
with her mind
each fighting the
other
her heart slaying
every time.

-N.R.Hart

Old Soul

Her heart
is not like
other hearts...
it beats in rhythm
to her old soul...
still believing
in love
in passion
in romance.

-N.R.Hart

The anticipation of him
had her heart racing again...
he came towards her grabbing her
by the hair and pulling her into him
kissing her roughly, then softly
his tongue demanding of her
he was a bit of a tease
he liked watching her squirm
feeling her mounting desire
her body responding to his
every touch
he knew he was in control of her
and her pleasure
his skilled hands moving as her body
arched under him
she was completely under his spell
as she whispered for him not to stop
but, he wouldn't be satisfied until
he heard her beg to be taken by him
and, then he knew it was time
for he couldn't wait a minute longer
either...to take her, to have her
to love her.
The sweetest surrender of all.

    -N.R.Hart "sweet surrender"

To the girls
soft and wild
their jasmine hearts
swell at a lover's
unyielding touch
delicate bodies
begging for
the crush
of your hard body
ravish them
a bouquet of wildflowers
for they want only
to love and be loved
by you. -N.R.Hart

Twin Flames (part2)

Twin flames are two souls bound
together by familiarity and forged
by fire.
They are continually drawn and pulled
towards one another in mysterious ways
through the universe that defy time, space,
gravity and return to each other again
and again like the powerul tides
of the ocean.
You feel each other so strongly,
so intensely, that it can scare you off...
an emotional roller coaster of feelings
on every level, mentally, spiritually,
soulfully and physically that goes beyond
explanation.
Trying to leave each other alone and
fighting this fiery bond between souls
with this "oneness" will only
strengthen and seal it for all eternity.
It is a love like no other...
One you will not likely experience again
in this lifetime. —N.R.Hart

"the memory of us"
You can pretend you don't notice
pretend you don't see
as you pass by all our favorite
spots
the familiar stop lights
and street signs, the winding
roads and all the miles we have
traveled
our lips touching
our hearts racing
our bodies on fire
our souls imprinted
with a wild love
too rare to lose
too addictive to quit.
You can run far my love,
but the memory of us will always
turn you back around. -N.R.Hart

What a mess you made
of things
trying so hard
to convince yourself
you aren't in love
with her anymore.

-N.R.Hart , what a mess

Undone

Love me until
I am in pieces
coming apart
at the seams
I need to come undone
in your hands
do not leave me here
untouched.
                        -N.R.Hart

wingman

He was always there watching
and waiting
keeping the wolves at bay
he was someone she could tell
her secrets to
and she knew they were safe
with him.
And, while all the others left
even as she whispered softly
how she needed them so
He stayed...
without her having to say a word.
He stayed because he wanted her
in his life no matter what.
And, if she were to fall
he would be there to carry her
until she was ready to fly again
because sometimes,
a girl just needs a wingman too.
N.R.Hart, Wingman

And, will you remember
my love, will you?
The crushing force
of my kiss
as we steal the same
breath
you dwell within my soul
living inside of me
You will have to tear me
open...
to break free.

N.R.Hart , You Dwell Within My Soul

WARRIOR PRINCESS (PART2)

She was a warrior princess
she fought until the very end
for love
because a true queen
picks her battle's wisely
she knew when it was time
to lay down her sword,
To give up the fight
and save herself instead.

— N.R. HART

"I do not profess to know all there is
to know about love, but I do know this;
bringing back the romance in life...
in love...is necessary for us to "feel"
again, to become softer in this hard
world.
To be a little more human again.
Poetry is necessary in order for us
to feel our souls again."

*"They say romance is dead...well,
then I am here to bring it back to life."*

-N.R.Hart, "Poetry and Pearls" ©

An Autumn Season

"I am an old soul trying
to survive in a modern world."

N.R.Hart

I am a romantic,
a dreamer,
an old soul trying to
survive
in a modern world.
I dwell in hope.
I walk in moonlight.
I live amongst the stars.
I want someone who
understands.
Someone who speaks the
same
language I do. Love.

—N.R.Hart "a Romantic"

FALL FROM GRACE

I wrote you in as
a superhero a fairytale
a beast
your eyes your lips
your hands
saving me again and again
loving me back to life.
When you went away
something in me died that day
and you were just a man
once again.
A beast that was once a friend.

A man that was once a legend.

N.R. Hart, A Legend

"This thing we have
goes beyond reason
it's our souls
fighting for us
even when our eyes
couldn't see."

-N.R.Hart

beyond reason

a love letter to my lover

I love no one but you. you are my sun
and moon. you are every star in the
sky.
you are my spring romance,
my summer day, my winter night,
my autumn love.
you are all my seasons.
how i love you in ways i don't even
understand. i need to show you my love.
i have saved so many kisses
just for you
for i have never felt this way before.
there is never enough time.
there is never enough you.
i close my eyes and all i see is your
face. all i crave is your touch.
my heart pounds for you and only you.
i love you. i am in love with you.
i ache for you. there is always a part
of me waiting for you. i am never not
waiting for you. until next time...

                -N.R.Hart, a love letter

Every Beast needs
his Beauty
the one who always
believed in him
when no one else did.

N.R.HART.

N.R.Hart, Beauty and her Beast ©2019

Love's greatest tragedy

Love's greatest tragedy isn't anything loud
or obvious...but rather, it is the quiet,
little tragedies of love.
The small moments we live for, the moments
we no longer get to see, the ones now lost
to us.
Maybe we all have that "one"...
we are unable to speak of...to think of them
makes your heart hurt with so many memories.
The one who meant so much to us.
The one who made us feel more than we've
ever felt. And, when we allow our minds
to drift and remember their smile or
the color of their eyes, we can actually
feel the physical pain of our heart breaking.
It's always there...these tiny memories...
the things we miss the most.
They live inside of us now, still so alive.
Still so big. Still so haunting...
And now, the small things become the big
things. Because, the biggest tragedy
in love is in all the missing. So much
missing of small, quiet things. -N.R.Hart

"Muse"

When they ask me
about you
I will tell them this.
You were the only boy
I loved so hard
that it broke me.

   -N.R.Hart

Muse

Does it frighten you...that I won't
write for you anymore or worse,
it won't be about you...
especially when you think about
me as much as I think about you.
Such a privilege for a poet to pen
their thoughts of another human.
When we are both gone my words
and your memory live on.
Maybe this is about you or...
maybe I will write something new.

N.R.Hart

Sacred heart

Why are we so fearful of love
of vulnerability,
of being human...
that we avoid getting close to
others,
not telling them how we feel
as if we are protecting
something sacred
like our own hearts.
Our hearts are sacred
because they are filled
with so much love.
Because love isn't worth
anything
if you don't give it away.
It is a wasted love.
Be brave in love.
Do not fear loving too much.
Fear not loving enough.
Fear that.   -N.R.Hart

159

Something beautiful

Maybe it's not about the words.
Maybe she has too many words she
can't even begin to write in her
head.
Maybe it's the fact that she
never stops trying even when
the right words won't come...
she writes them anyway.
There is something fragile
in that.
There is something brave
something beautiful...
in that.
          -N.R.Hart

The Girl with The Pen

You won't write
the ending
to our love story
You don't hold
that kind of
power
But I do...
You must have
forgotten
who you are
dealing with...
I'm the girl
with the pen.

-N.R.Hart , The Last of the Romantics

"I did it for love" by N.R.Hart

And, if you were
to ask me
why I did it
why I do
everything...
well, the answer
is simple,
I did it for love.

-N.R.Hart

Translate Love

You don't know this but I now
understand why you were sent to me.
You gave me the adventure of a
lifetime...
and for that I will always
love you the most.
Maybe you were sent to me for
a higher purpose.
Maybe it was for me to translate love...
to the people.
Maybe it was for me to translate love...
to the rest of the World.

-N.R.Hart

And just like her eyes
there was a large love
trapped inside
and the biggest tragedy
her life...
she couldn't live
her love ...
she couldn't give it all away
She was held captive.
-N.R.Hart

"The power of love"
And, love looked like
a girl wearing a crown
of flowers and the wind
blowing through her hair.
And, love looked like
a girl with innocence
in her eyes and a heart
full of butterflies.
And, love looked like a girl
with hopeful hands and a beautiful
soul.
And in the end, love looked like
a girl who lived for love and died
for love.
A queen who made entire kingdoms
fall...
They were no match against the
power of love, after all. -N.R.Hart

You thought you could forget
about us.
You thought you could
untwist untie undo this love...
but this love was already entwined
within us...
we were soul deep...in love.
our souls loved one another
long before we ever knew.
This love was a once in a lifetime
love...
one we cannot undo.
god, how I knew.

N.R.Hart "soul deep"

Soul language

I used to feel oddly out of place
feeling things ever so deeply,
so intensely...
which made me think I was too different,
too sensitive and more alone
than everyone else who seemed to
ordinarily go about their day without
staring into someone's eyes
just to feel them or find comfort in
human connection, in human vulnerability.
I was always grasping for something that
I could not put a name to. I wanted more,
I needed more...than small talk and
shallow connections.
A longing deep inside to be heard.
An ache to feel understood.
Until one day I finally discovered that
you just can't talk soul language...
with superficial people. -N.R.Hart

Superpower

Why do we try to
fit in where we do
not belong to become
like everyone else?
I belong only to myself.
Be yourself.
There is no one
like you in this world.
And, that alone
is your superpower. —N.R.Hart

What about her?

The world needs people
like you they told her...
it needs your pure heart
it needs your softness
the world needs for you
to remind us about love
again...to bring us back
to ourselves again.
You are the lovers of this world
a world that so desperately
needs to feel your kind of
love again.
But, what about her...
She was too busy trying
to save the world
who was going to save her?

      -N.R.Hart

Hurricane

I had the wind
knocked out of me
today...
after I picked myself
back up I decided
I'd become
the fucking hurricane
instead.

-N.R.Hart

Wildflower soul

N.R.Hart

Rest now
wildflower
soul
if no one
has told you
today
you are so
strong
and brave
and beautiful
fighting for
them
fighting for
love
I am so
proud of you
rest now
wildflower
soul
the world
can wait.

Pages of Poetry

Dried flowers pressed
between these pages of poetry
marking a before and after
a cherished love
a precious romance
as the forget-me-not
he loves me, he loves me not
petals keep falling
and I am still falling...
heavy with longing.
How did love die
in-between these lines?
The beautiful agony
the beautiful ache
of love.

                    -N.R.Hart

broken things

You can never go back
to the person you were
before
the pain and the heartbreak.
The pain changes you.
It changes who you are.
Maybe you are guarded now.
Maybe you don't trust
as easily.
Maybe you are a little more
broken.
Pain changes the person
you used to be.
The innocence of love
is lost...
But, you still love. You still love.
And, you learn that broken
things... deserve love too.

N.R.Hart, broken things

dragon heart

She's got a dragon
heart
the way she loves
is fire
always fire
and she will consume
you
in her flames.

N.R.Hart dragon heart

QUEEN OF HEARTS

THEY CALL ME THE
QUEEN OF HEARTS
I FOUGHT TO THE DEATH FOR LOVE
I FOUGHT FOR US...
YOU WERE MY SWORD-HEARTED
 LOVER
ONLY TO FIND OUT YOU WERE NEVER
 BUILT FOR WAR. YOU RAN INSTEAD.
YOU LOST THE QUEEN. CHECKMATE.
AND, YOU NEVER GOT THE GIRL
IN THE END.

N.R.HART, QUEEN OF HEARTS

Broken heart

They say you can feel a pain
in your heart
almost like it is breaking in two
because of the hollow feeling
inside of missing someone.
Your breathing doesn't feel
quite right like there is no air
or maybe you are holding
your breath
or not breathing at all.
Because your soul
is crying out
because your heart knows
something is missing.
Because it only hurts...
when you breathe. —N.R.Hart

You think you have time so you wait...
yet, what are you waiting for. The right time?
There is never a right time...there is only now.
Were you thinking you had forever? Because, we
are all just living on borrowed time.
You never know which day will be your last.
I try to live life that way. Like it could be
my last day here on earth. So I don't want to
wait...not for anything.
I send that text that I wrote, telling you that
I miss you. If I want to see you then nothing
can stop me. I say how I am feeling before the
feeling passes...because the moment will be lost
forever. How many moments have been lost in love?
Life is about feelings and feelings are desperate
things. They are messy things. Realize that and
be desperate, be brave. Come undone.
Live in the moment. I know of no other way. Tell
people you care about them. Kiss them. Love them.
Tell them you can't live without them. You never
know when you will have the chance again.
Time is precious. Do it now. —N.R.Hart

Not all of us can
be "Romantics"
they told her
and she answered
back oh, but
they must!
Life can be so
dreadful without
it.   —N. R. Hart

"She wanted a soul
like hers...
ancient, restless
wild
eternally forged in
love, skin and fire."

-N.R.Hart

Romantic Tragedy

Is this a death wish
when it comes to love?
I have this insane desire
to want everything all
at once,
break my own heart, offer my soul
for the taking.
Is this my own romantic tragedy?
So be it.
If I must go down, let it be
in love and legacy.
-N.R.Hart , The Last of the Romantics

"So, gather up your brilliant
and shining pieces
you will show them
how broken becomes beautiful." N.R.Hart

Someone once told me to get my head
out from the clouds and asked
why are you so romantic
about...everything?
The answer was simple. Why would I
want to come back down to earth...
so much pain and sadness here
I stay up where the beauty lives.
Just maybe this world needs more
poets and dreamers...
if we can take your pain away
for just a moment and make you
believe in something again...
we bloom love and passion
we sprinkle hope and stardust
we plant flowers in souls and
watch beautiful gardens grow.

N.R. Hart

"sprinkling hope"

I was always there for you
I held your hand
and never let go because
I knew you needed it.
You needed me.
I listened to your dreams.
I loved all of them.
I loved you.
I held on to you like
a daydream
like a habit
like I would be doing it
forever....
But, when my hands reached
for you
because my hands were always
reaching for you
you let go...just like that...
Just when I needed you most.

N.R.Hart "I Needed You Most"

182

Speak to me in poetry
give me
beautiful tragedies
written in verse
sweet sonnets written
in rhyme
soliloquies in poetic
little vignettes
romance me
with your words
seduce me
with your verbs
love me with your lines
speak to me in poetry
it's the only language
I am fluent in.

N.R.Hart, "Speak to me in poetry"

Just the thought of
never seeing you again
can this be the end
of everything?
Never feeling your hand
touch mine
or your lips kiss mine...
How can this be true?
Forever is such a long time
without you.

N.R.Hart, Forever is a Long Time

Remember me

Remember my heart.
Remember how I loved you.
Remember me as the softest
whisper of your soul.
Remember me.

                    -N.R.Hart

"Wild Creature"

You can tell your heart
a million different
things
you can tell it
to feel this way
or that way
but, the heart wants
what it wants...
and in the end,
the only thing
it will believe in...is love.
Only love. Always love.

-N.R.Hart, The Last of the Romantics

My mind had nothing
to do with it.
My soul chose you.

-N.R.Hart "soulmate poem"

Love is not
logical
it will
make you
do things
you wouldn't
normally do
crazy things
terrible things
beautiful things.

N.R.Hart, The Last of The Romantics

You will remain both
the villain and the hero
in my love story.
My tragedy and my fairytale.

N.R.Hart , The Last of the Romantics

Downfall

So many romances
dancing around
in her head
the heart of a
dreamer
she is pure love
that was her charm
that was her
downfall
that was her
destiny.

-N.R.Hart

She said in a pleading whisper,
please don't go...
I will miss you so.
But, he left anyway
there will be someone like her again.
Until it finally hit him...
there will never be another her.
His heart...hurt.
His soul was in a constant state
of unrest.
He spent the rest of his life
searching for her.
But, he never found her.
Not ever again.

N.R.Hart "another her"

"Burning roses"

She is one of the rare ones who puts love before
everything else. She relies on her heart
speaking to her. And, sometimes it is screaming
at her. To follow love, to follow her heart,
to follow her soul.
Many are intimidated by her fire, she is a
turbulent piece of earth, not many get to stand next to.
To be around her is to understand love.
They are the lucky ones.
They can feel her pulse, her energy, her passion.
She is a pure light.
You become childlike again in her presence.
There is a sense of urgency with her.
She is a wild star about to take flight.
A romantic with a pounding heart. She doesn't wait for
tomorrow, it may never come. She lives in the moment.
A flurry of butterflies. She wants love and hope and you
and now and now. And, those that have been loved by her
can still smell the smoke.
She leaves a trail of burning roses behind her.
For she believes only in poetry and love and passion
and everything she can feel and cannot see.
She remains a universe of secrets. Her heart a hidden
mystery. With poems yet to be written.
She is her own heroine. Her own love story.
She will write her own ending.
You see, she romanticized everything in her life.
She made it beautiful again. -N.R.Hart

Hopeless Romantic

And, in the end I want
to be remembered
as the hopeless romantic
who fought for love...
who believed in love.
The one who was in love
with love.

-N.R.Hart©

Heroes, part II

There will be that one person
in your life
that loves you like no one ever has
or will
they will love you so unconditionally
with all their energy...all their soul
how they sacrificed and surrendered
every part of themselves
that it may have even scared you.
And, oftentimes you won't realize
until much later in life...
who this person was.

-N.R.HART

The Last of the Romantics, "Heroes part II" 2020

Seasons of the heart

We are the Winter Roses
the sleeping twilight.
We are the Flowers of Spring
the dying rain.
We are the summer stars
the melting moonlight.
We are the Autumn leaves
the falling, the crashing.
The chill will kill you but
the burn is sweet.
Always follow your heart...
the Seasons of your Heart.
Oh, how we tremble for love...
again and again.

-N.R.Hart, Seasons of the heart

ABOUT THE AUTHOR

N.R.Hart started writing poetry at a young age and used her poetry as a way to express her innermost thoughts and emotions. A true romantic at heart, she expresses feelings of love, hope, passion, despair, vulnerability and romance in her poetry. Trapping time forever and a keeper of memories is what she loves most about the enduring power of poetry. Her poetry has been so eloquently described as "words delicately placed inside a storm." Poetry is here to make us feel instead of think; as thinking is for the mind and poetry is for the heart and soul. N.R.Hart hopes to open up your heart and touch your soul with her poetry.

"Poetry is not dead, it is alive
in the minds of those
who feel...instead of think."

N.R.Hart

Connect with N.R.Hart:
Facebook@N.R.Hart, Author
Facebook@PearlsSlippingOffAString
Instagram@nrhartpoetry
Tumblr@nrhartpoetry